Change Makers

THE MAGIC NUMBERS

A Handbook on the Power of Math and How It Has Transformed Our World

Hoe Yeen Nie

Illustrated by David Liew

Change Makers was created with Hwee Goh
who continues to provide oversight for this series.

© 2022 Marshall Cavendish International (Asia) Pte Ltd
Text © Hoe Yeen Nie
Illustrations © David Liew

ISBN 978-981-4974-39-4 (Hardcover Edition)
ISBN 978-981-5066-03-6 (Paperback Edition)

Published by Marshall Cavendish Children
An imprint of Marshall Cavendish International

All rights reserved

No part of this publication may be reproduced, stored in a retrieval system or transmitted, in any form or by any means, electronic, mechanical, photocopying, recording or otherwise, without the prior permission of the copyright owner. Requests for permission should be addressed to the Publisher, Marshall Cavendish International (Asia) Private Limited, 1 New Industrial Road, Singapore 536196. Tel: (65) 6213 9300
E-mail: genref@sg.marshallcavendish.com
Website: www.marshallcavendish.com

The publisher makes no representation or warranties with respect to the contents of this book, and specifically disclaims any implied warranties or merchantability or fitness for any particular purpose, and shall in no event be liable for any loss of profit or any other commercial damage, including but not limited to special, incidental, consequential, or other damages.

Other Marshall Cavendish Offices:
Marshall Cavendish Corporation, 800 Westchester Ave, Suite N-641, Rye Brook, NY 10573, USA • Marshall Cavendish International (Thailand) Co Ltd, 253 Asoke, 16th Flr, Sukhumvit 21 Road, Klongtoey Nua, Wattana, Bangkok 10110, Thailand • Marshall Cavendish (Malaysia) Sdn Bhd, Times Subang, Lot 46, Subang Hi-Tech Industrial Park, Batu Tiga, 40000 Shah Alam, Selangor Darul Ehsan, Malaysia

Marshall Cavendish is a registered trademark of Times Publishing Limited

National Library Board, Singapore Cataloguing in Publication Data

Name(s): Hoe, Yeen Nie. | Liew, David, illustrator.
Title: The magic numbers : a handbook on the power of math and how it has transformed our world / Hoe Yeen Nie ; illustrated by David Liew.
Other Title(s): Handbook on the power of math and how it has transformed our world | Change makers (Marshall Cavendish Children)
Description: Singapore : Marshall Cavendish Children, [2022]
Identifier(s): ISBN 978-981-4974-39-4 (hardback) | 978-981-5066-03-6 (paperback)
Subject(s): LCSH: Mathematics--Miscellanea--Juvenile literature. | Mathematical ability--Juvenile literature.
Classification: DDC 510--dc23

Printed in Singapore

CONTENTS

1. Ready? 1, 2, 3! 4
2. Let Me Count Thy Ways 10
3. From Zero to Hero 12
4. The Amazing Numbers 18
5. Measuring the World 24
6. The Age of Reason 30
7. From Ada to AI 37
8. Numbers That Rule 45
9. When Math Goes Wrong 51
10. Welcome to the Crypto Future 59

My Ideas Matrix 66
Yeen's Handbook Toolkit 68
Acknowledgements 70
About Yeen and David 71

READY? 1, 2, 3!

Counting is the first and simplest form of math. But strange as it may seem, there was a time when counting and numbers didn't exist. How was this possible?

A Very Useful Bone

No one knows when and how early humans learnt to count, but it probably began many thousands of years ago with the use of fingers. Later, to count bigger quantities, someone decides to use a monkey bone, and carves 29 neat lines into it. This bone, found in Africa in the 1970s, is 40,000 years old and one of the oldest mathematical tools ever discovered.

Did You Know?
A 30,000-year-old counting stick, made from wolf bone, has 55 cuts arranged in groups of 5. Archaeologists say this may be related to the 5 fingers of a hand.

Write It Down!

Around 4,000 BC, the Mesopotamians were using small clay objects to represent quantities like 1, 10 and 60. But as their cities grew, they needed a better system to keep track of people, cattle and grain. They had a brilliant idea: using their **cuneiform** script, they created numbers! This meant they could easily count into the thousands, and record taxes and trade.

What's That?
Cuneiform is the world's first writing system. Its name means "wedge shaped". Read the next chapter to find out why!

Did You Know?
Besides writing, the Mesopotamians also invented the wheel and agriculture. That's why the area, located in modern Iraq, is called the Cradle of Civilisation.

Did You Know?
The first name ever written doesn't belong to a king or a warrior, but an accountant, Kushim! It appears on a clay tablet from 3,000 BC that recorded a business deal.

Nine Useful Symbols

For much of history, civilisations used words, letters or pictures to represent numbers. But this made even basic math complicated. In the 7th century, the Indians developed a set of simple symbols that made complex calculations much easier to do. It was truly a **game changer**. The invention spread to the Middle East and Europe, and it's how we write 1 to 9 today.

What's That?
A **game changer** transforms a situation in a big and positive way.

Did You Know?
The ancient Indians loved math, and invented rules for multiplication, division and square roots, still in use today.

Square roots? Hmm, I don't know. Have you considered switching from gardening to math?

Count Like a Babylonian

60 seconds in a minute, 60 minutes in an hour, 360 degrees in a circle. When we measure time or angles, we are using an ancient number system. Babylonian mathematicians 4,000 years ago loved the number 60 because it could be divided by 1, 2, 3, 4, 5 and 6. Babylonian math may have disappeared from our modern world, but you can still see it whenever you look at the clock.

How Many Is That?

The Warlpiri tribe in Australia only has words for "1", "2" and "many", while the Pirahã in Brazil have no number words at all. Instead, they say "small amount", "large amount" or "many". Others count without number words. In Papua New Guinea, the Yupno can go up to 33, by pointing at body parts such as fingers, toes, eyes, ears and nostrils.

Did You Know?
Chicks, fish and chimpanzees can recognise the difference between big and small. They can even count and do basic sums!

Is Equals To = ARGH!

In 1557, Welsh mathematician Robert Recorde was working on his algebra textbook, *The Whetstone of Witte*, when he got fed up with writing "is equals to" over and over again. Back then, math was written out in full sentences, so no wonder he was annoyed! Recorde's solution was to invent a new symbol =. He used two parallel lines because "no two things can be more equal".

> **Did You Know?**
> Ancient Egyptians described addition and subtraction by drawing a pair of legs. If the feet pointed to the right, it meant addition. Feet pointing to the left indicated subtraction.

How did other math symbols come about?
- The +, for addition, originates from the Latin word *et*, that means "and".
- Some believe the –, for subtraction, comes from a symbol used by merchants. It was made popular by German mathematician Johannes Widmann in 1489.
- The multiplication symbol, x, is first used by English mathematician William Oughtred in 1631, and based on the Cross of Saint Andrew.
- The division sign, ÷, has a name: obelus! It's an ancient Greek word that means "sharpened stick", and the sign represents a small dagger. It is first used in math in 1659.

LET ME COUNT THY WAYS...

These are some of the ways
ancient civilisations wrote their numbers.

Y	1	∏	2	∭	3	⩑	4	⩑	5
(	10	(T	11	(∏	12	(⩑	15	((	20

Mesopotamians

The Mesopotamians' number system
was written in cuneiform. They used
v to represent 1 and < to mean 10.
So how would you write 23 in cuneiform?

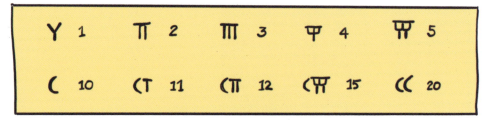

Egyptians

The ancient Egyptians used a number system
based on 10. Their written script was called hieroglyphs,
and they had a symbol for 1, 10, 100, 1000,
up to 10 million. How would they write 12,413?

α	β	γ	δ	ε	ϛ	ζ	η	θ
1	2	3	4	5	6	7	8	9

Greeks

The ancient Greeks adapted the 24 letters of their alphabet and created 3 more. These 27 letters were used to represent values 1 to 9, 10 to 90, and 100 to 900. Here's what 1 to 9 looks like.

1	2	3	4	5	6	7	8	9	0
૧	૨	૩	૪	૫	६	७	८	९	०

Indians

This script is an early version of the numerals many of us use today. In the 7th century, it spread to the Arab world where it continued to evolve. Notice that this is the first ancient script to include a 0.

Answer:

12,413 in hieroglyphs is

23 in cuneiform is

FROM ZERO TO HERO

The invention of the number 0 caused a revolution in math. But for centuries, people in Europe were afraid of it, calling it evil. So how did this oval-shaped digit go from math villain to hero?

When Nothing Didn't Exist

Since ancient times, people have understood that 0 means "nothing". But they couldn't imagine 0 as a number, like 1 or 7. If there is nothing there, how can you count it? The Babylonians and Mayans had symbols for 0, but only to show the difference between 5 and 50, or 12 and 102. Even the Greeks, ancient masters of math, didn't need 0. That's because instead of numbers, they used letters and diagrams for math (page 11).

Much Ado About Nothing

It was in India that 0 finally became a number. In 628, the astronomer Brahmagupta was the first to explain how you could add it, subtract it, even multiply it.* The invention spread to China and the Middle East, and in the 9th century, the Persian scholar al-Khwarizmi used 0 to create a new branch of math called algebra. He also suggested the digit be drawn as a circle. He called it *sifr*, meaning "empty".

> **Did You Know?**
> In algebra, you move parts of an equation around to balance it. That's why its original Arabic name is *al-jabr*, meaning a "reunion of broken parts"!

> **Did You Know?**
> Al-Khwarizmi also came up with methods to quickly multiply and divide numbers. We call them "algorithms", after his name. (Try saying both aloud!)

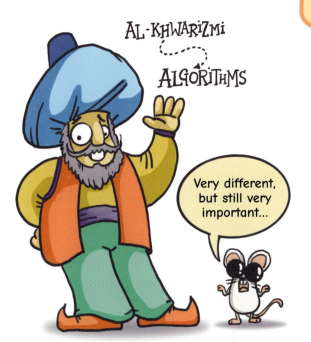

*__Note:__ Brahmagupta said, "When 0 is added to a number or subtracted from it, the number remains unchanged. A number multiplied by 0, becomes 0."

A Dangerous Idea

While the Hindus in India accepted the concept of "nothing", for Christians in medieval Europe, "nothing" meant an infinite empty space. This terrified them, and they called 0 dangerous and evil. In 1299, 0 was even banned in Florence, Italy, though for a different reason. The Florentines thought 0 could encourage **fraud**, as 0 could be altered to become 9 or added after a number to increase its value.

Did You Know?
It's said that ancient Hindus were comfortable with 0 because the concept of "nothing" was deep in their philosophy. Their word for it, *shunya*, is still used today.

What's That?
fraud: An act of deceit and dishonesty.

Did You Know?
Despite the ban in Florence, merchants continued to use 0 in secret. Its Arabic name, *sifr*, led to the word "cipher", which has come to mean "code".

HOW CAN 8 CHOCOLATES BE EATEN BY ZERO PEOPLE?

A Very Strange Number

If you divide 9 chocolates by 3 people, each person gets 3. But what if there are 0 people? How do you share among 0 people? This is one example of 0's strangeness — you can't divide by 0! This unusual feature is the basis of calculus, a very important area of math. Calculus describes how anything changes over time, even changes so tiny, they approach 0 size. It is used to **forecast** the future, from stock market performance to the spread of a virus.

Did You Know?
The number 0 is neither positive nor negative, but it is an even number. This is because when divided by 2, it produces a whole number, even if the answer is 0!

What's That?
To **forecast** is to predict an outcome after careful study.

0 < or > 1?

For humans, learning about 0 takes extra brain power, effort and time. When neuroscientists asked young children to name the smaller number between 0 and 1, most of them picked… 1! Even adults will hesitate before giving the right answer.

What's That?
A **neuroscientist** is someone who studies the human brain.

Did You Know?
When scientists repeated the experiment on bees, they found that the insects gave similar results as the humans. This is impressive considering that bees have tiny brains less than 1 milligram! Bees are amazing in many other ways.*

*See Change Makers: Little Big Heroes

Don't worry! At least YOU can make honey!

Hero of the Modern World

What would today's world look like without 0? Well, we would not have important fields of science and technology such as physics, engineering and economics. Imagine, no cars, electricity or space exploration. Even computers would not exist! The programming language that drives computer systems, binary code, is made up of 1s and 0s. 0 impacts every part of our lives, and that's why it is considered one of mankind's greatest inventions.

THE AMAZING NUMBERS

Now that you've been introduced to the strange world of 0, here are some other numbers that seem to have special, even magical, properties!

The Rule of 3

The ancient Greeks saw it as a perfect number, while the Swedes and Koreans believe it brings luck. Today, some of the most memorable slogans come in sets of 3 — "Yes We Can", "Just Do It", "I Came, I Saw, I Conquered". Studies show our brains love patterns, and the smallest number the brain identifies as a pattern? 3! When things are in 3s, we remember them better.

> **Did You Know?**
> Famous 3s in literature include the 3 witches in Shakespeare's Macbeth, the 3 musketeers... and of course, the 3 blind mice!

> **Did You Know?**
> The number 3 also describes a triangle, which is considered the strongest and most stable shape.

As Easy As Pi

Pi, or π, is the ratio of a circle's circumference to its diameter. With it, we can build bridges, arches, even the Pyramids of Giza. It's also used in physics, astronomy and math. What's really cool about pi is that it is infinitely long. Since Babylonian times, people have sought to find all the digits of pi. In 2021, Swiss researchers used high speed computers to calculate up to 62.8 trillion decimal places, a feat that took 108 days and 9 hours. Thankfully, most of us just use 3.14!

> **Did You Know?**
> In 2015, Rajveer Meena of India set the world record for the most pi digits ever recited — 70,000! He took 10 hours, and wore a blindfold throughout to prove he wasn't cheating.

> **Did You Know?**
> March 14 is known as Pi Day, because the date is written as 3.14. And how do people around the world celebrate? By eating pie, of course!

The Fairest Number of All

There's a special number said to be responsible for nature's most beautiful patterns — 1.618, or phi (ϕ). Better known as the "golden ratio", phi is closely related to the **Fibonacci sequence**. The spiral of seeds in the centre of a sunflower, the arrangement of leaves and petals in some plants, and even the ratio of female to male honeybees in a hive — these are some elegant examples of the golden ratio in action.

What's That?
The **Fibonacci sequence** is an endless series that begins with 0, 1, 1, 2, 3, 5, 8, ... and continues by adding the last 2 digits to get the next.

Did You Know?
In the 12th century, the Italian mathematician Fibonacci came up with his famous sequence while trying to solve the question — how quickly can rabbits breed in a year?

*Pisa Society for the Prevention of Cruelty to Animals

Did You Know?
Some believe the golden ratio exists in masterpieces such as Leonardo da Vinci's Last Supper and the Pantheon in Athens, or even in proportions of the human body! But scientists say this is a myth, a false idea.

Optimus Primes

A prime is a whole number that can only be divided by 1 and itself. In 300 BC, Greek scholar Euclid proved that there is an infinite number of primes, a fact that makes modern **encryption** possible. We can easily multiply 2 large primes to make a super-huge number, but no computer can work backwards quickly enough to figure out what those 2 primes are. It's like a code that's impossible to crack! Each time we make an online purchase or send a protected email, prime numbers keep our data safe.

What's That?
encryption: To keep data secure using math techniques.

Did You Know?
The only even prime number is 2. All others are odd.

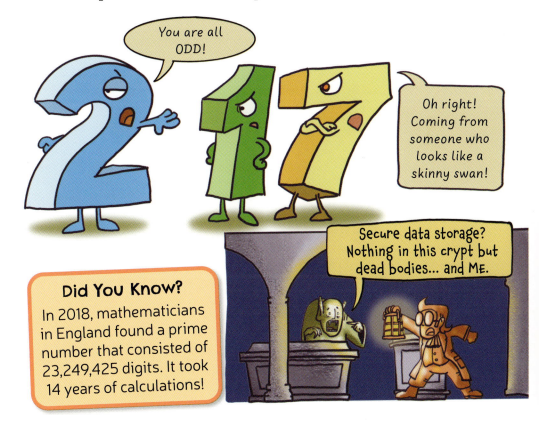

Did You Know?
In 2018, mathematicians in England found a prime number that consisted of 23,249,425 digits. It took 14 years of calculations!

Just My Imagination?

Imagine a number that, when multiplied by itself (or squared), gives a negative number. Huh? Yup, welcome to the world of imaginary numbers. But while they seem unreal, these special digits have many practical uses. With imaginary numbers, engineers and scientists can study electrical currents as well as how things move, such as light and water. This lets them work out how earthquakes shake buildings, and how to build better (and smaller) electronic devices, and create mathematical models to forecast the weather.

Er... Hi Mum...
About this report card...
Don't worry about it...
The numbers are IMAGINARY!

Did You Know?

If the idea of imaginary numbers seems crazy and strange, remember that 1,500 years ago, people were just as confused by the invention of 0!

MATHEMATICS DEPARTMENT

Not Crazy, Just Irrational!

Not only can numbers be imaginary, they can also be irrational! No, they are not crazy, irrational just means they cannot be written as a simple ratio or fraction. Greek philosopher Pythagoras had discovered their existence 2,500 years ago. He was so shocked by the idea that he called irrational numbers "unutterable". If any of his followers revealed them to the public, they would be put to death!

Did You Know?
Pythagoras believed in the magical qualities of whole numbers and their ratios, and formed a secret cult devoted to the study of math.

Did You Know?
Pi and phi are both irrational numbers. Although we commonly write pi as $22/7$, it is not entirely accurate, simply a close estimate.

MEASURING THE WORLD

The size of Earth, the length of a minute, the speed of light. Some of the most basic measurements of our world were first calculated with simple tools, combined with flashes of **ingenuity**. How did people do it? And how did the math they create lay the foundation for modern life?

> **What's That?**
> **ingenuity**: Being extremely clever and original.

A Way to Measure Everyday Life

5,000 years ago, ancient Egyptians and Mesopotamians were devising ways to measure the lengths, areas and volumes of physical objects. Much of it was to help with everyday life — to decide the size of land, build pyramids and houses, and store oil and grain. Later, the Greeks called this "geometry", after *geo* ("Earth") and *metreon* ("measure").

Did You Know?
Euclid, who lived in 300 BC, is called the "father of geometry". His *Elements* is one of the most influential textbooks ever written, and is still studied today.

Did You Know?
The most famous geometric formula is Pythagoras' Theorem, $a^2 + b^2 = c^2$. In the past, cartographers used it to measure heights and distances to create maps. In modern times, it is the foundation for GPS.

A Stick and a Shadow

Today, with satellites and GPS, we can easily calculate that the Earth's circumference is 40,075 km. But 2,000 years ago, the Greeks had already worked it out, using just a stick! Eratosthenes assumed the Earth was a sphere of 360 degrees. He knew of a well in Syene city where the sun shone straight down each **summer solstice** at noon. That same day, he stuck a pole in Alexandria city, 800 km away, and at noon measured the degree of its shadow — 7 degrees. If 7 degrees = 800 km, then 360 degrees = 41,000 km. Bingo!

What's That?

Summer solstice is the day in June when the sun is at its highest point in the sky and daylight hours are the longest.

Did You Know?

Ancient Greeks and Egyptians measured large distances by walking between places while counting their steps.

1,012,349...
1,012, 350...
Hey, what's that?
...Oh! Argh!
1... 2... 3...

Your pole won't happen to have a night mode, would it? I have to work late tonight.

CARTOGRAPHER

Did You Know?

Eratosthenes made one of the world's earliest known maps of Earth. He divided it into 5 climate zones, including the 2 freezing Poles. He also gave us the word, "geography".

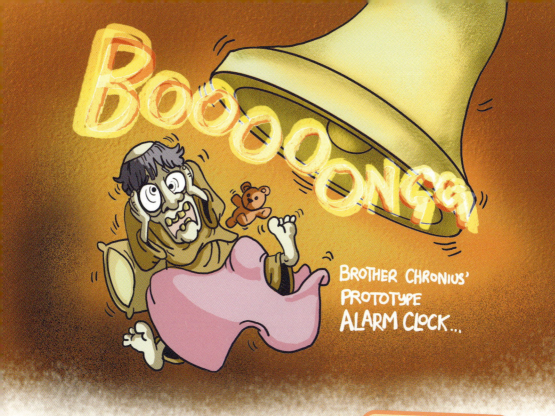

BROTHER CHRONIUS' PROTOTYPE ALARM CLOCK...

Hickory Dickory Dock

The earliest clock was the sundial, based on the shadow created as the sun moved through the sky. Later came the water clock, which marked time by the regular drip of water. But something more accurate was needed that would not be affected by cloudy days or freezing weather. In 1656, Dutchman Christiaan Huygens solved the problem with a pendulum clock. At last, time could be measured not just in hours, but minutes and seconds too.

Did You Know?
"Clock" comes from the Latin word for bell, *clocca*. Bells were used to signal prayer times for Benedictine monks.

Did You Know?
The most precise modern clocks are atomic clocks which measure the energy emitted by an atom or molecule. Their accuracy makes satellites, computer networks and GPS tracking possible.

Math on the High Seas

In the past, to be a good sailor, you had to know math. To navigate or work out your position on the seas, you used trigonometry — by observing the sun, moon and stars, and measuring their angles and distances to the horizon. But a tiny error meant ships became hopelessly lost. With the invention of reliable clocks in the 17th century, navigators could accurately calculate their speed and positions. This enabled more ambitious ocean voyages.

Did You Know?
Trigonometry is also used by virtual game developers to design a character and make it move within a space.

Did You Know?
Trigonometry remains a useful skill for modern navigators. It was one of the tools used by NASA astronauts in the 1960s to go to the moon. NASA's moon voyage* changed our view of Earth.

*See Change Makers: Little Big Heroes

The Mystery of the Moon

In 1676, Danish astronomer Ole Roemer was studying the **orbit** of one of Jupiter's moons when he discovered something strange. Sometimes the moon's eclipse — when it went behind Jupiter — would happen sooner than predicted, sometimes later. Roemer realised this depended on Earth's position. When it is further from Jupiter, light from the moon travels a longer distance to reach us. We see the eclipse later. From his observations, Roemer calculated the speed of light. Although incorrect, it was the first real measurement of light ever made.

What's That?
orbit: The curved path taken by a moon around a planet.

Did You Know?
In 1983, using laser techniques, the speed of light was finally defined as 299,792,458 metres per second.

Did You Know?
Before the 1600s, some thought light travelled instantaneously. For them, it explained why we see objects the moment we open our eyes.

THE AGE OF REASON

The European **Renaissance** (1200s–1600s) was a time of excitement over learning and discovery. New continents were found, the printing press* was invented, and art and commerce flourished. Above all, great progress was made in math and science.

*See Change Makers: Railroads to Superhighways

> **What's That?**
> **Renaissance** (rerh-NAY-sonse) is a French word meaning "rebirth". It refers to renewed interest in ideas of ancient Greece and Rome.

*A fancy way of saying "therefore".

Abacus Schools

In medieval Europe, math wasn't as widely respected as subjects like Latin and philosophy. But in the 13th century, as global trade grew, "abacus schools" emerged in Italy to teach the sons of wealthy merchants how to run a business. Interest rates, profit and loss, and reading and writing were among the practical subjects taught. Abacus schools also allowed the poor to get an education.

> **Did You Know?**
> Abacus schools were named after the Latin word, *abaco*, which means "to calculate".

Math Duels

From the 16th century, the rise of printed math textbooks in Europe made the sharing of ideas much easier. It also made math super competitive. Scholars would hold public contests, challenging others to solve incredibly difficult math problems. Winners gained fame and fortune, while those they defeated might even lose their careers.

> **Did You Know?**
> Such competitions have spurred innovations in mathematical thinking over the centuries, and continue to be held today.

WHEN BRAWN TRULY WINS OVER BRAINS...

I guess it's true, nobody likes a gloating math nerd.

A 300-Year-Old Puzzle

Can you prove there is no solution to $x^n + y^n = z^n$ for $n > 2$? Don't worry if you can't! This is Fermat's Last Theorem, the most famous math puzzle in history. French mathematician Pierre de Fermat issued the challenge in 1657, but it was so difficult that it wasn't solved until 1995, by British mathematician Andrew Wiles. By then, so many attempts had failed that people thought a proof could not exist!

Did You Know?
Fermat is known for many contributions to math, but he was a lawyer by profession. Math was only one of his many hobbies.

Did You Know?
Wiles was only 10 when he became fascinated by Fermat's Last Theorem.

Move It Like Newton

In his 1687 masterpiece, the *Principia*, Isaac Newton not only describes how gravity works, he also comes up with Three Laws of Motion to explain how things move:

- A moving object will keep going unless another force acts on it, such as gravity or air resistance. That's why when you kick a ball, it eventually comes to a stop.
- The greater the mass of the object, the more force you will need to move it. Think about how much easier it is to push a chair than a large wardrobe!
- For every action, there is an equal and opposite reaction. When a tennis ball hits the ground, the ground applies an equal force, causing the ball to bounce up.

Did You Know?
Why do objects always drop straight down? Why not sideways? That's what Newton wondered when he saw an apple fall to the ground. This thought later became his theory of gravity.

Did You Know?
Why don't we fall out of our seats when we go upside down on a rollercoaster ride? It's because of a special kind of force called "centrifugal force".

MAMA NEWTON HELPING A YOUNG ISAAC DEVELOP HIS LAWS OF MOTION.

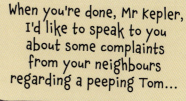

The Path of the Planets

During the Renaissance, people made important new discoveries about the universe. One key figure was the 16th-century astronomer and mathematician, Johannes Kepler. He calculated that the planets move in an ellipse, a shape that's like a squished circle. He also showed that instead of orbiting at a constant speed, planets moved faster when nearer to the sun, and slower when further away.

Did You Know?

Kepler was the first to explain how a telescope works. He also designed spectacles to treat myopia and long-sightedness.

Did You Know?

People once believed that the sun and planets revolved around Earth. The 15th-century Polish astronomer Nicolaus Copernicus was the first to argue that it was actually the sun that lay at the centre of the solar system.

Math Tricks the Eye

We admire great artists like Leonardo da Vinci for their realistic paintings. What's their secret? Math! During the Renaissance, the desire of artists to represent the natural world accurately led them to study math, and geometry was especially useful. These painters developed perspective techniques to depict human proportion, portray scale, or to create the illusion of 3-dimensional (3D) space on flat canvas.

> **Did You Know?**
> Trompe l'oeil is a famous type of 3D illusion. On ceilings, these "deceptions" give the effect of infinite space. In a painting, they can fool us into thinking we're looking at the real thing!

Fun Fact: The Red Cross became a symbol of protection in 1864.

FROM ADA TO AI

The history of the computer goes back even further than we think: to the 1830s. In the 200 years since, people have invented machines that can perform complex tasks, outsmart enemies and even imitate human behaviour. At the root of all these innovations, is math.

*Wingdings: A typeface where the letters take the form of symbols.

Babbage's Super Idea

In the 1830s, the English mathematician Charles Babbage was working on a super calculator when he came up with an even better idea. This was basically the world's first computer, and he called it the Analytical Engine. Just like a modern computer, Babbage's machine would have a Central Processing Unit (CPU), and could be programmed to do tasks. Sadly, the Analytical Engine was too advanced for its time and never got built.

Did You Know?
Babbage's machine would have been powered by steam because this was before the invention of electricity!

The First Programmer

The world's first computer programme was created by a brilliant mathematician, Ada Lovelace. She wrote it in 1843 for the Analytical Engine using binary code, a mathematical series of 0s and 1s. The data was entered on cards punched with holes. These "punched cards" continued to operate computers until the 1970s, while binary code is still used today.

Did You Know?
Lovelace also believed that the Analytical Engine could create music based on math rules and make new math discoveries.

Did You Know?
Lovelace's father was Lord Byron, a famous English poet. Her mother encouraged her love for math, even though women had few opportunities in science in the 1800s.

To Outsmart and Outwit Them All

What comes to mind when you think of codes and spies? James Bond? High-tech gadgets? How about… math? Code making (and breaking) involves logical thinking and even some simple addition and subtraction. The Roman Emperor Julius Caesar used a code where, instead of A, he would write D, three letters forward in the alphabet (+3). To decode a message, his soldiers had to find the letter that was 3 places behind (–3).

Cracking the Enigma

During World War II, the Germans built a code-making machine called Enigma that was nearly impossible to outsmart. That was because it could create 158,962,555,217,826,360,000 different code combinations, or nearly 159 million trillions! But in 1940, British mathematician Alan Turing* uncovered Enigma's secret, allowing him and his codebreakers to decipher enemy messages. At one stage, they were intercepting and decoding 2 messages every minute. Their work changed the course of the war.

> **Did You Know?**
> Work at Britain's code-breaking unit at Bletchley Park was kept top secret until the 1970s. Till then, few were aware of Turing's role.

> **Did You Know?**
> Turing was also a pioneer of **AI (Artificial Intelligence)**. He created the "Turing test" to assess if a computer can "think", based on its ability to successfully imitate human conversation.

> **What's That?**
> **AI (Artificial Intelligence)** refers to a computer or programme that is built to 'think' and respond like a human.

*See Change Makers: Railroads to Superhighways

Armies of Computers

For centuries, computers weren't machines, but people! Their job was to solve simple equations as part of a larger team making complex calculations. They crunched numbers on astronomy and navigation, and, during World War II, improved the accuracy of missiles. After the war, NASA hired teams of skilled women computers. One of them was Katherine Johnson, and it was her groundbreaking math that sent American astronauts into space and later, to the moon.

> **Did You Know?**
> The word "computer" has its roots in Latin. It means "to think" and "to calculate". Until the 1970s, it was still used as a job title... for a person!.

> **Did You Know?**
> Human computers at NASA did all their calculations by hand, on pen and paper. Solving, or computing, a problem could take days of work and fill stacks of notebooks.

The Trillion Dollar Equation

In 1998, an American computer science student found a way to make internet searches faster and more accurate. Today, Larry Page's creation, Google, is used by much of the world. But the math that powers the search engine's **algorithms** is ancient. It's based on something called matrix theory, and similar methods were used by Chinese mathematicians over 2,000 years ago. Little-known equations can be used to transform technology and the way we live.

What's That?

An **algorithm** is a set of rules that a computer follows to solve problems.

Did You Know?

Matrix theory is now used in the study of neural networks to help researchers develop AI technology that mimics the way our brain works.

ANCIENT CHINESE MATHEMATICIAN/ VISIONARY

The Math Behind the Magic

From virtual reality to talking robots and self-driving cars, AI might seem like magic. But really, it's just math. For instance, to build a self-driving car, you need to calculate uncertainty: that's probability (*see* page 46). Linear algebra helps scientists solve problems around speech recognition, while geometry and trigonometry are needed to build realistic virtual reality worlds. It's math that creates the magic behind all great tech innovations.

> **Did You Know?**
> In 2015, YouTube engineers used the concept of "gradient descent", developed by a 19th-century French mathematician, and increased the time users spent watching YouTube videos by 2,000 per cent.

NUMBERS THAT RULE

Whether we realise it or not, much of our everyday lives is secretly determined by numbers — from how long we can live, to how many friends we can have. In our modern tech-filled world, this is perhaps Nature's way of reminding us who's boss!

What Are the Odds?

It's been calculated that the chances of you (or me) being born is 1 in 400 trillion. It's a number so tiny, the fact that we exist at all feels like a miracle. Mathematicians prefer the word "probability", the likelihood of a random event happening over time. Here are a few examples:

- If you have 23 people in a room, there is a 50 per cent chance that 2 of them will share the same birthday.
- Boys born in 2010 have a 25.7 per cent chance to live till 100. Among girls, it's 33.3 per cent.
- The odds of being struck by lightning in your lifetime are 1 in 15,300. Being killed in a plane crash? 1 in 11 million.
- Winning the lottery is even more rare. The odds of that are 1 in 292 million.

> **Did You Know?**
> Probability began as a tool to study gambling and insurance. Along with statistics, it's now used to analyse economies and populations, and in other social sciences.

Can We Be Immortals?

In 1900, the average person lived to about 30. Today, thanks to improved medical care and better lifestyles, most of us reach 70 quite easily. But can we live forever? Well… nature says no. Our bodies can heal themselves from injury and illness, but scientists have found that this natural ability stops around the ages 120 to 150. In future, we might discover ways to reprogramme ageing cells or create mechanical organs to help humans live beyond 150.

Did You Know?
Worldwide, there are over 500,000 centenarians, people who live to 100. Supercentenarians, those who live beyond 110, are very rare. Most of them are in Japan.

Did You Know?
The oldest person who ever lived is Jeanne Calment (1875–1997) of France. She died at a grand old age of 122 years and 164 days.

Six Degrees of Separation

In a world of 7.7 billion people, imagine being connected to the Queen of England or the Pope — or to me! — through just 6 other people! Well, the theory of "6 degrees of separation" says the world is smaller than you think. And in 2008, researchers found proof. Using a database of 30 billion online messages, they connected 180 billion pairs of strangers through an average of 6.6 other people. Today, with social media, linking up the world is even easier.

Dunbar's 150 Friends

Social networks have made it easier to make friends, but how many do we need anyway? According to British **anthropologist** Robin Dunbar: 150! Blame our brains. Dunbar discovered that based on the size of our brains, we can have meaningful relationships with at most 150 people at any one time. What's more, his theory says we would consider only 50 of them as friends. Good pals? 15. Best friends? Just 5.

What's That?
An **anthropologist** studies what makes us human, from our body and behaviour, to our culture and language.

Sorry, Oggbogg. Nothing personal, but we can't be friends because you're number 151... You'll cause civilisation to collapse...

Awww...

Did You Know?
Dunbar developed his theory while studying monkeys and apes. He found that the bigger their brains, the larger their social group. Applying the ratio to humans gives 150.

Did You Know?
The rule of 150 is true for early hunter-gatherer societies, as well as modern groupings like offices and social networks. Any larger and the bonds start to weaken.

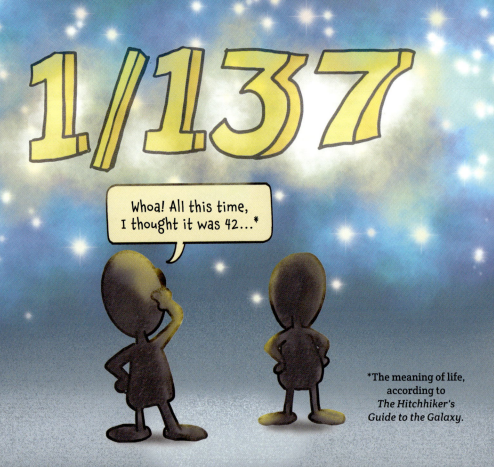

*The meaning of life, according to *The Hitchhiker's Guide to the Galaxy*.

The Key to the Universe

There are some numbers that are incredibly important in explaining how our universe works. One is the speed of light. Here's another: $1/137$. Scientists don't know where this number comes from, but it pops up in many important physics formulas. For instance, $1/137$ specifies how strongly particles stick together. If its value was even a tiny bit bigger or smaller, atoms and molecules will not form. In other words, neither Earth, nor you and I would exist!

Did You Know?
In physics, particles such as electrons and protons stick — or "bond" — together using a force called electromagnetism.

WHEN MATH GOES WRONG...

Math has enabled humans to do incredible things. We've invented intelligent machines and even flown people to the moon. But the big secret of math is that humans are not very good at it! Some of our errors make life a little more interesting, but others come with more serious consequences.

The Power of 99

Ever notice how the prices of many items end with 99? Say, $4.99 or $299. Is it a math trick? Not really, it's **psychology**. Selling a product at $4.99 instead of $5 makes us think the price is closer to $4, even though the real difference is only $0.01. This works with prices ending with 9, too. In a university experiment, a dress was marketed at $34, $39, and $44. The one priced at $39 sold the most, and compared to the cheapest option, sales were 24 per cent higher!

What's That?
Psychology is the scientific study of how our mind influences our behaviour.

Did You Know?
When US department store JCPenney changed prices to get rid of 9, sales dropped by 28 per cent. Its motto was, "No games, just great prices", but it seemed that shoppers actually preferred the game.

The "Magic 9s" don't always work ...

The Bigger, Better Burger

In the 1980s, the American fast-food chain A&W launched a burger to compete with McDonald's Quarter Pounder. Called the 1/3 Pounder, it was bigger and sold at the same price. Good deal, right? But no one bought it! Turns out, customers weren't great at fractions. They thought 1/3 was smaller than 1/4, when it was the opposite. Thanks to bad math, A&W's experiment was a flop.

Did You Know?
A&W fixed the problem by renaming the burger "The Papa Burger". Sales went up after that.

The Walkie Scorchie

In 2014, a London skyscraper, nicknamed the "Walkie Talkie" for its shape, became the "Walkie Scorchie" when engineers miscalculated the angle of its glass exterior and turned it into a giant **concave** mirror! When the sun hit the glass on a bright day, its intense rays were reflected onto its surroundings, burning pavements, bicycle seats and even cars. Since then, a sunshade has been added to solve the problem.

What's That?
A **concave** surface curves inwards, reflecting and focussing light onto a single point.

Did You Know?
The Walkie Talkie had another problem. Due to its design, strong winds get pushed down the tower's walls, creating downdrafts mighty enough to blow people onto the street and knock signs off nearby buildings.

Too Many Numbers

4 June 1996. The Ariane 5 rocket blasts off towards space, only to explode 39 seconds later. Thankfully, no one was onboard. What happened? The computer had gotten its math wrong. Every computer has limits on how much data it can process at a time. But there was a **software bug** in the Ariane 5 that miscalculated. As the rocket accelerated, an enormous amount of data was produced, far too much for its system to handle. In response, it self-destructed, and the US$370 million rocket went up in smoke.

What's That?
A **software bug** is an error or fault in a computer system that causes it to produce a wrong or unexpected result.

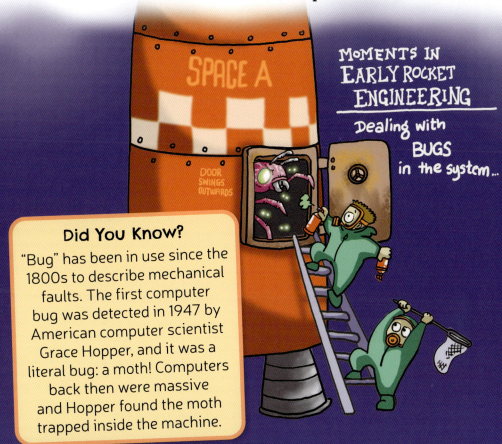

MOMENTS IN EARLY ROCKET ENGINEERING

Dealing with BUGS in the system...

Did You Know?
"Bug" has been in use since the 1800s to describe mechanical faults. The first computer bug was detected in 1947 by American computer scientist Grace Hopper, and it was a literal bug: a moth! Computers back then were massive and Hopper found the moth trapped inside the machine.

Help! It's Y2K

In 1999, the world was thrown into a panic as the new millennium (year 2000) approached. Why? Because of a coding problem — the Y2K bug! Back then, the year was shortened to the last two digits in computer programmes to save memory space. People feared that on 1 January 2000, the computers would think it was 1900. Systems would crash, and banks, power plants and government records would fail. Countries spent US$300 billion to upgrade their computer systems, and 1 January 2000 arrived without a glitch — to a huge sigh of relief.

Did You Know?
Y2K did cause some problems. In New York, a video store charged a customer for returning a rented movie 100 years late. The bill? US$91,250!

Did You Know?
In 2012, a similar coding error led to a Swedish woman being asked to enrol in preschool. Problem is, she was born in 1907, not 2007!

Give Me Five!

In Germany, a political party must win over 5 per cent of votes to enter Parliament. And in a 1992 election, 5 per cent was exactly what the Green Party won. But in reality, their vote share was 4.97 per cent. The computer had rounded it up to 5.0! Once this was discovered, the Greens lost their seat. A simple rounding error had changed the outcome of an election.

Not-So-Smart AI

AI can be trained to solve all types of problems, except — surprise, surprise — math! A team of scientists taught an AI machine to do hundreds of thousands of math sums, but when tested, it got 95 per cent of answers wrong. No one has yet figured out why, and till they do, this limits AI's usefulness in math-based scientific research.

WELCOME TO THE CRYPTO FUTURE

Metal coins, seashells, strips of leather and paper… throughout history, money has come in all shapes and sizes. In recent years, thanks to math, a new form of currency has been created, one that exists entirely on the internet. Could cryptocurrency be the future of our world?

> **Did You Know?**
> Money's value used to be linked to gold or silver, but now we use "fiat money". This means its value depends on our trust in governments, which have the power to print currency and regulate its use.

The World's most secure currency… Stone discs from the Yap Islands

A Big Idea

In 2008, computer programmer Satoshi Nakamoto has a game-changing idea: bitcoin, a new currency that exists entirely online and isn't regulated by any government or central bank. What makes it extremely secure is a technology called blockchain, which uses math-based encryption to protect information. When you pay someone using bitcoin, the system confirms the transaction by using computers to solve complex math problems. The first computer that succeeds also gets rewarded with new bitcoins.

Did You Know?
Satoshi Nakamoto's identity is a mystery. No one knows whether the creator of bitcoin is a he or she, or even if it's an individual or a group of people.

Did You Know?
Bitcoin is the best known cryptocurrency, but it's not the only one. Today, there exists about 18,000 different cryptocurrencies.

Cryptocurrency is very real.. but the REAL question is... AM I REAL?

Crypto's Climate Change Conundrum

Solving these math puzzles is the only way to create — or "mine" — new bitcoin. But these require powerful computers that use up a lot of energy. Much of it is generated using fossil fuels, leading to criticism that cryptocurrencies are worsening climate change.* The race to mine crypto is also wasteful, as equipment is constantly upgraded for faster, more efficient machines.

*See Change Makers: The Earth Experiment

What's That?
conundrum: A problem that is difficult to deal with.

Did You Know?
A single bitcoin transaction burns about 2292.5 kilowatt hours of electricity, enough to power a household in the US for 78 days. In a year, it uses more energy than the Netherlands.

The Power of Musk

In February 2022, electric carmaker Tesla started accepting dogecoin for merchandise like belt buckles and children's bikes. This was announced on Twitter by Tesla's billionaire founder, Elon Musk, and the news sent dogecoin's value shooting up. Musk is one of crypto's most famous supporters, and his comments on social media often have enormous impact on the value of virtual currencies.

Did You Know?

Dogecoin was created as a joke in 2013. It was named after a **meme** that was popular at the time, of a Shiba Inu dog.

What's That?

meme (meem): An image or video that goes viral online, often with users writing their own funny captions.

The Almost Multi-Millionaire

We've all forgotten passwords before, but what if the password unlocks a giant fortune? Years ago, when bitcoin's value was low, Stefan Thomas was paid 7,002 bitcoins for creating a video. Now his stash is worth over US$260 million, but without his password, Thomas can't get his money! So far, he has tried and failed 8 times to unlock the code on his hard drive. If he gets it wrong another 2 times, he can say bye to his treasure forever.

Did You Know?
Each bitcoin owner has a private key, or password, generated by encryption. It's nearly impossible to decode as there are more combinations than there are atoms in the universe.

Did You Know?
It's estimated that about 3.7 million bitcoins are "lost" because their owners have forgotten their passwords. Their total value? About US$150 billion.

Not Fungi, But Non-Fungible

Would you spend US$250,000 on a drawing of a rock, US$3 million on a tweet, or even US$69 million on an online video? Welcome to the crazy world of non-fungible tokens, or NFTs. No no, this has nothing to do with mushrooms. NFTs are pieces of data stored on the blockchain that enable digital content to be bought and sold. Can anyone copy or download the same online image? Yes. But the buyer of the NFT is given a "token" that proves they own the "original" work.

What's That?
Non-fungible means an object is unique and not easily replaced. A $100 note is "fungible", but a house or old photo is not.

Psst! Wanna make a fortune? Just pay me $1 million for this digital fungus!

Did You Know?
Supporters say NFTs help digital artists, but others believe it is a gimmick that won't last.

The Real Change Maker?

Beyond cryptocurrencies and NFTs, could blockchain be the real change maker? Due to its hard-to-crack, math-based encryption technology, many believe blockchain can be extremely useful in our daily lives.

- Keeping public information, such as identity numbers and medical records, on a blockchain is safer than existing database systems, which are easier to **hack**.

- Blockchain can improve the security of the billions of smart gadgets that are connected to the internet, such as alarms systems, jet engines or home appliances that we control with apps.

> **What's That?**
> **hack**: To access data in a system or computer without permission.

MY Ideas MATRIX

Dear Reader,

With each turn of the page, we hope you've enjoyed discovering the magic of numbers, meeting mathematical minds of the past, and learning how they have transformed our world.

Which was your favourite story? Why not find out more and write down what you've learnt on these pages?

Or how about inventing a secret code so you can swop messages with your friends? Or challenge yourself to memorise as many digits of pi as possible?

Stay curious and enjoy the journey!

Love,

Yeen & Shiew

YEEN'S HANDBOOK TOOLKIT

Can you imagine a world without math?
I certainly can't, and I hope that by now, neither can you.
But if you still need a little more convincing, here are
5 more reasons we all need math in our lives!

Math Is a Basic Survival Skill

Whether it's measuring ingredients or changing
the proportions of a recipe, math is essential
in the kitchen. You need it too when you go
shopping, so you know how much you can spend,
and if the cashier has given the right change.
Plus, math can help you spot a good discount!

Math Teaches Us to Think Better

In ancient Greek, the root word of mathematics
is "learning". In Hebrew, it's "thinking". Any knowledge
is readily available on the internet, but the real skill
is in how we analyse the information, raise questions
and seek evidence, while keeping an open mind to
new ideas. Math trains us to learn and think logically.

Math Is Good for Your Brain

A Stanford University study found that children who know math are also better at making decisions and paying attention. Our brains use the same regions for these functions, so do more math to build those brain muscles!

Math Is a Universal Language

An equation doesn't need to be translated to be understood by someone on the other side of the world. Neither do the laws of math change just because 2 people have a different religion. Wherever you are, 2 + 2 = 4. This makes math a powerful tool for sharing ideas.

Math Is Beautiful

Bees use hexagons to build their honeycombs; flowers arrange their petals according to the Fibonacci sequence; and repeating patterns, called fractals, are found in snowflakes and river networks. Nature is full of the beauty of math, we just have to keep our eyes wide open!

ACKNOWLEDGEMENTS

Isaac Newton once said, "If I have seen further it is by standing on the shoulders of giants." Likewise, I have benefitted greatly from the writings of brilliant science and math communicators who set out in clear, simple language the math concepts and ideas that this book draws on.

A huge thank you to Lydia Leong and Hwee Goh for trusting an arts student to write a book on math.

And also to Pierpaolo and Luca, my constant companions.

ABOUT YEEN AND DAVID

Hoe Yeen Nie is an award-winning documentary filmmaker and TV journalist who enjoys telling stories that reveal unexpected truths about ourselves and the world we live in. Trained in the humanities, she nonetheless has a long-held love for math and remembers "Three Is the Magic Number" as a favourite childhood song. Follow her @yeennie.hoe.

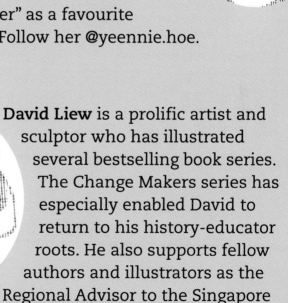

David Liew is a prolific artist and sculptor who has illustrated several bestselling book series. The Change Makers series has especially enabled David to return to his history-educator roots. He also supports fellow authors and illustrators as the Regional Advisor to the Singapore chapter of the Society of Children's Book Writers and Illustrators.

Numeric or Exponential?

Did you see that? Numbers ARE magic!

If they can do the same to my block of cheese, now THAT would be magic!